YOUR KNOWLEDGE HAS VALUE

Bibliographic information published by the German National Library:

The German National Library lists this publication in the National Bibliography; detailed bibliographic data are available on the Internet at http://dnb.dnb.de .

Imprint:

Copyright © 2019 GRIN Verlag
Print and binding: Books on Demand GmbH, Norderstedt Germany
ISBN: 9783346089540

This book at GRIN:

https://www.grin.com/document/504832

Washington Mutwiri

Home Security Systems. Intrusion Detection with GSM

GRIN Verlag

GRIN - Your knowledge has value

Since its foundation in 1998, GRIN has specialized in publishing academic texts by students, college teachers and other academics as e-book and printed book. The website www.grin.com is an ideal platform for presenting term papers, final papers, scientific essays, dissertations and specialist books.

Visit us on the internet:

http://www.grin.com/

http://www.facebook.com/grincom

http://www.twitter.com/grin_com

GSM HOME SECURITY SYSTEM

Inhaltsverzeichnis

Introduction

In the current era of modern technology, the issue of home security is paramount as the burglars advanced their intrusion techniques using various applications of cutting-edge technology. The need to secure our homes arises due to due to the need to protect various important documents, property, and life. This has necessitated the development of intelligent systems that are implemented through application-based technologies to automate home security systems. The Idea of Intelligent homes is based on digital systems such as wireless technologies that are fitted with Artificial Intelligence Systems to perform certain predetermined tasks. The AI systems provide the homeowners with real-time feedback and are able to respond accordingly to various security concerns. The advancement in technology has been responsible for the development of digital home security applications allow for real-time communication and emergency response by monitoring factors such as temperature and home lighting. The automated home security systems additionally secure homes by integrating the automated user-authentication software that prevents break-ins and track illegal intrusions within and around the home.

There various advanced intelligent home security applications operating in with different systems. However, this report focuses on an effective, practical, and economically efficient GSM module integrated with IR sensors. This system is designed to detect intrusions and respond through alarm systems that restrict entry by activating various lock mechanisms to secure the premises. The system functionality of this embedded home security application is integrated with facial recognition software and Artificial Intelligence technology such as voice detection and motion sensors. The functionality of this system is easy to understand thus the users do not require advanced knowledge and skills in Information Technology. The system is user-friendly in terms of power consumption, maintenance, optimization, and allows for device interoperability.

The Relevant Background

The proposed home security system integrates various components and subsystems of the IR sensors into a specially designed GSM module to come up with a functional single automated architecture that functions effectively in a wide range of intelligent home environments (Isa and Sklavos, 2017). The figure below illustrates the architecture diagram of the home security system with the design set up and connectivity of its various modules.

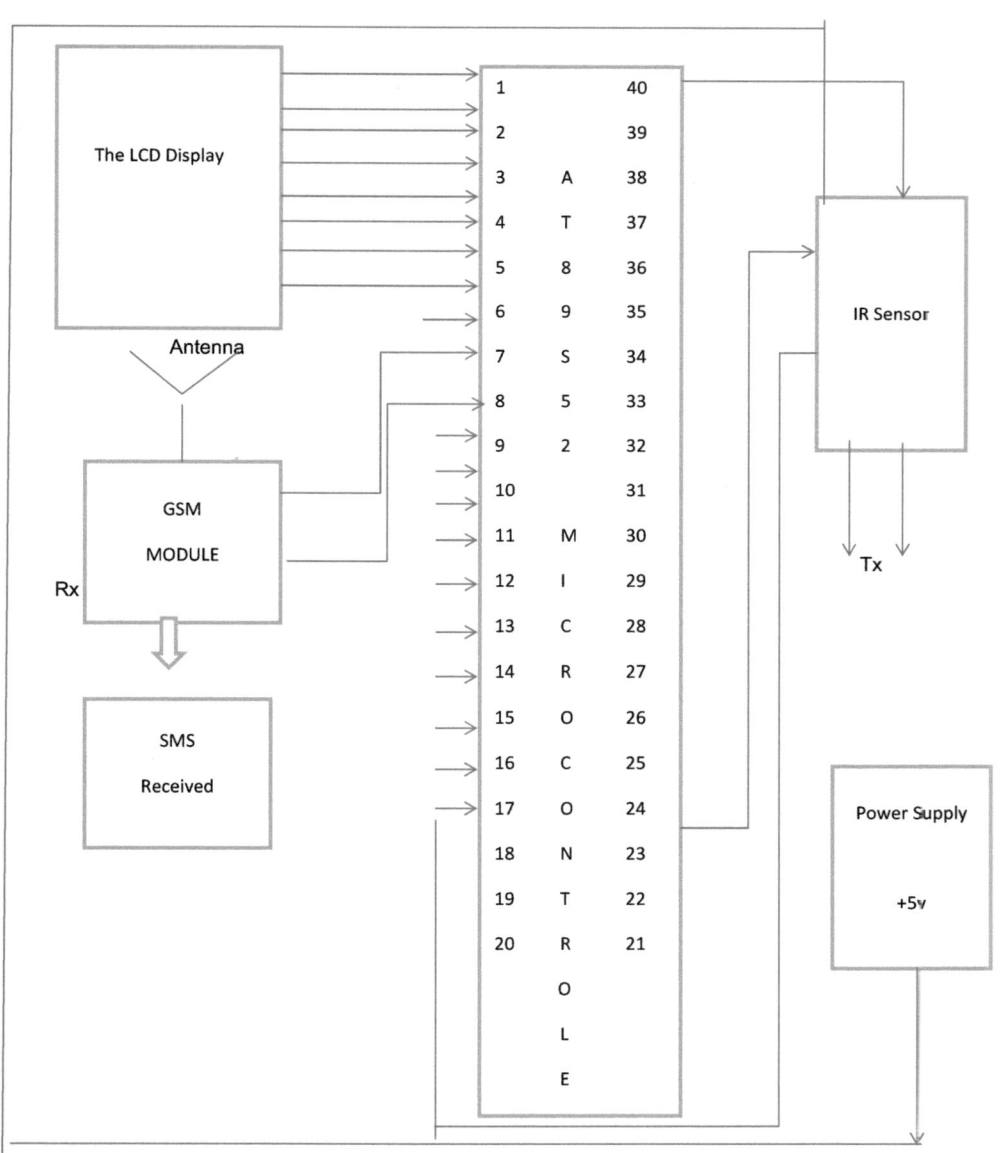

Summary of the components
AT89S52 Microcontroller

This is a high-performance 8-bit Microcontroller with a built-in programmable memory of 8K bytes. This Highly effective CMOS device is designed using advanced technology that incorporates high density and non-volatile storage memory that is easily compatible with the 80C51 instruction set that is commonly used as the Industry commercial standard. Moreover, the flash memory contains an on-chip flash that makes it possible to reprogram the inbuilt memory to suit user needs in a wide range of home environments (Hasan et al., 2015). The ATS9S52 Microcontroller is among the most efficient embedded solutions that are sufficiently flexible and cheap. Moreover, this microcontroller can be integrated into a wide range of embedded control systems.

The Key features of the Microcontroller

- A flash memory of 8K bytes

- Random Access Memory of 256 bytes

- Two data pointers

- One On-chip oscillator

- 32 Input-Output lines

- Operating range of between 4.0V to 5.5v

- Multiple 16-bit timers

- A complete duplex serial port

- 6-vector double interrupt design

The Liquid Crystal Display

This is a thin electronic visual display that makes use of various properties of the liquid crystals such as the modulation to display information. The LCDs are widely used in most display applications due to their portability, compactness, reliability, affordable prices, and little or no impacts on the eyes. Compared to the traditional Cathode Ray Tubes, the LCDs are more reliable with regard to energy efficiency and ease of disposal. The low power consumption makes the LCD display compatible with electronic devices that are battery powered.

The Infrared Sensor

These are important components of the intelligent home security system. They are composed of the Infrared emitter and the Infrared receiver. When an infrared emitter is connected to a power source, it emits the infrared rays that are synthesized by the infrared receiver which is connected to the voltage divider (Parab and Joglekar, 2015). The Infrared sensor works on the basis of voltage resistance such that when an infrared beam of high intensity is directed to the infrared receiver, the resistance of the receiver reduces thus reducing the output voltage in the divider. Moreover, when the distance between the infrared emitter and the receiver is increased, the intensity of the infrared decreases as long as the sensor and the reflecting service are within a fixed distance.

The Light Emitting Diodes

These are the devices used to provide electronic lighting to facilitate the functioning of the light sensors. The LEDs have low energy consumption, compact size, durable, reliable, and are more robust. However, the Light Emitting Diodes to supply sufficient lighting for a room are quite expensive and may need specific current and heating requirement compared to the common fluorescent sources of light that produce equal output (Parab and Joglekar, 2015).

The GSM module

This refers to the Global System for Mobile device that is composed of a SIM900 Quad-band General Packet Radio Service (GPRS) device that operates on frequencies ranging between 850MHZ to 1900MHZ. This device is portable and can be easily plugged in a GSM modem which is designed using 3V3 and 5V Direct Current interfacing circuitry that makes it possible for a user to have a direct interface with a wide range of microcontrollers used in the home security system (Yuksekkaya et al., 2006). This device is designed such that it's relatively easier to configure the baud rate within the range of 9600 to 115200 bps using the attention commands. Through the TCP/IP stacks, the GSM TTL modem can be connected to the internet using a GPRS application. This makes it convenient for sending messages and data transfer using the mobile application interface. To interface the GSM modem with the microcontroller, the Universal USART transmitter is used.

Features of the GSM module

- The Quad-band bandwidth 850-1900 MHz GPRS

- Internal RS232 Logic Converter

- An easy to Configure Baud Rate

- Internal Network Update LED

- 5-12V Input Voltage

MAX232 IC

This refers to an integrated circuit that is used to convert signals received from the RS-232 serial port into a more suitable signal that is compatible with the applicable logic circuits. Thus, the application can effectively function on the TTL logic and transmit data across all interconnected devices through a serial port (Parab and Joglekar, 2015).

The SIM card Slot

This is the Subscriber Identity Module that enables the User to access the services of a network provider through which the data shared from the GSM module can be easily transmitted over distances.

The figure below shows how the circuit will appear when the components are interconnected.

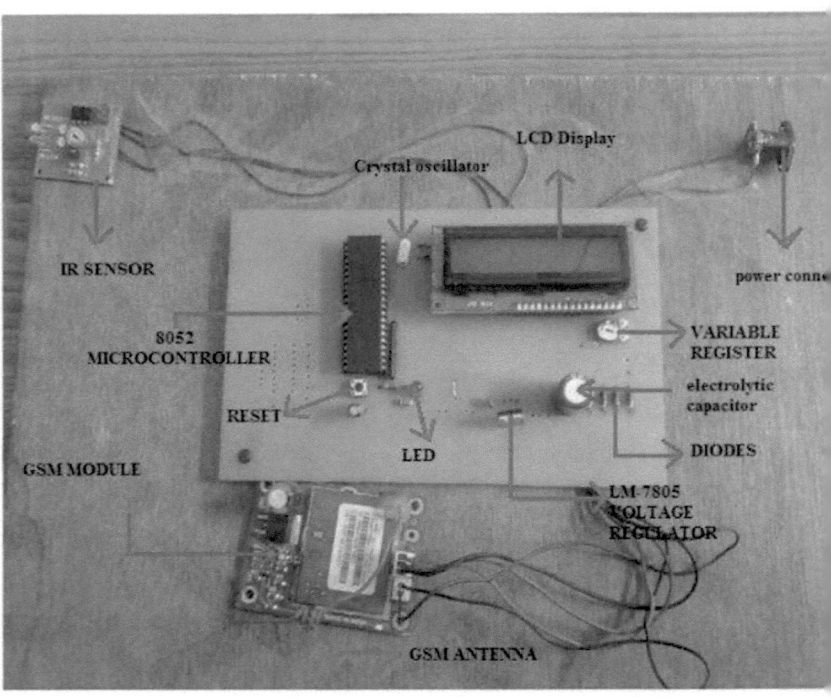

Methodology

The Infrared Sensor

The infrared sensor is designed to detect the obstacles that cross its beam of light and transmit the signal to the IR receiver immediately the radiation bounces back from the obstacle. Here, the infrared Light Emitting Diodes transmit an Infrared Signal towards a surface that reflects the signal back to the infrared receiver. The receiver may be made of a photodiode that decodes the infrared signal. Thus, when an obstacle obstructs the infrared beam, the circuit is broken and a signal is sent to the connected devices that initiate a response (Ragade, 2017).

The Infrared Transmitter

The IR transmitter functions by modulating the information signal to match the carrier signal since most of the off-shelf receiver modules are designed with a specified carrier frequency. Thus, it's important to ensure that the frequency of the receiver module matches the carrier frequency of the transmitter.

The Infrared Receiver

The infrared receiver used in this case is designed to transmit a 38 kHz signal that matches the frequency of the IC package. In this report, we will use the TSOP4838 IC package as the receiver module since it can easily be integrated with the TTL and the CMOS logic. This facilitates direct transmission of the digital signal to the receiver to the microcontroller (Teymourzadeh et al., 2013). After the transmitter and the signal receiver have a complete connection, they should be situated at a certain angle to ensure that obstacle detection takes place effectively. This angle should be +/-45° as the sensor directivity. The figure below shows how the sensor is directed.

This figure has been removed due to copyright issues.

It's important to ensure that both the infrared transmitter and the receiver have a thick enclosure to prevent the reflection of the IR radiation from the surrounding objects. This is important when focusing on unidirectional obstacle detection.

The Functionality of the GSM module

The GSM module utilizes the cellular technology in the wireless and wired data transmission. The wired connection receives data and the wireless connection that operates using the RF antenna transmits the text and voice data. This module used the Sim Card to communicate across the GSM standard network using the 3G mobile system (Khiyal, Khan, and Shehzadi, 2009). When the infrared sensor detects an object, it sends a signal to the microcontroller which directs the command to a GSM module. The Global System for Mobile Communications (GSM) transmits the signal informing of an SMS or voice data to a programmed mobile number in the microcontroller.

The final Design

The hardware and the software components of the GSM home security system are seamlessly integrated to provide the user with a real-time feedback on the security system by detecting the physical intrusions. The hardware components such as the connections between the microcontrollers, the GSM modules, the LEDs, and the LCD display is mainly through wired connections and the microchips that ensure a smooth flow of data from the infrared sensors to the user device across the GSM mobile system (Bangali and Shaligram, 2013). The software components that form the basis of internal programming are powered by the hardware components to facilitate the reception and transmission of data signals from the antenna.

The Strengths of the system

- The GSM security system has the capability to send automated reports to five re-set numbers through a mobile device to enable the user to monitor and communicate to the thief. Moreover, the system is made of eight security codes that can be armed or disarmed depending on the user needs (Zhai and Cheng, 2011).

- In the event of a security emergency, the GSM system is equipped with an SOS key on various devices such as the RF remote or surface sensors to send a signal to the connected devices in the form of a short message or voice call.

- Through the GSM system, a user can easily arm or disarm the reporting alarm system using an SMS command from a mobile device. Moreover, it allows for quick monitoring of the alarm status by sending an inquiry command to the main unit by SMS (Sharma et al, 2014).

- The GSM home-guard system has the power failure reporting functionalities set on a backup system to inform the user immediately the power goes off.

- The GSM security system utilizes global network technology that makes it system location independent of geographical barriers.

Design Evaluation

This home security design is highly reliable due to the low costs and ubiquitous accessibility from remote locations. The design was primarily selected due to its ability to auto-configure with most devices and diverse remote control abilities that increase its effectiveness as a security solution for homes compared to other systems. The components are cheap and easy to install. The entire GSM security system has low power consumption and high durability of its components. Moreover, the device can be optimized to cover different areas of security concern in its home-based application.

Conclusion

In this report, the GSM security system has been identified as the most reliable, convenient, and efficient solution for intrusion detection and real-time reporting. Due to the increasing security concerns, homeowners will have the best option for securing their homes by continuous monitoring and generation of security status reports using this security system. This system effectively functions on most mobile phone devices thus the users do not need to carry extra devices for monitoring the security situation at their homes. The system is cost-effective and durable thus the maintenance costs are reduced compared to other security systems such as the Arduino system.

References

Bangali, J. and Shaligram, A., 2013. Design and Implementation of Security Systems for Smart Home based on GSM technology. *International Journal of Smart Home, 7*(6), pp.201-208.

Hasan, R., Khan, M.M., Ashek, A. and Rumpa, I.J., 2015. Microcontroller Based Home Security System with GSM Technology. *Open Journal of Safety Science and Technology, 5*(02), p.55.

Isa, E. and Sklavos, N., 2017. Smart Home Automation: GSM Security System Design & Implementation. *Journal of Engineering Science & Technology Review, 10*(3).

Khiyal, M.S.H., Khan, A. and Shehzadi, E., 2009. SMS Based Wireless Home Appliance Control System (HACS) for Automating Appliances and Security. *Issues in Informing Science & Information Technology, 6*.

Parab, A.S. and Joglekar, A., 2015. Implementation of home security system using GSM module and microcontroller. *International Journal of Computer Science and Information Technologies, 6*(3), pp.2950-3.

Ragade, R.R., 2017, October. Embedded home surveillance system with pyroelectric infrared sensor using GSM. In *Intelligent Systems and Information Management (ICISIM), 2017 1st International Conference on* (pp. 321-324). IEEE.

Sharma, R.K., Mohammad, A., Kalita, H. and Kalita, D., 2014, February. Android interface based GSM home security system. In *Issues and Challenges in Intelligent Computing Techniques (ICICT), 2014 International Conference on* (pp. 196-201). IEEE.

Teymourzadeh, R., Ahmed, S.A., Chan, K.W. and Hoong, M.V., 2013, December. Smart gsm based home automation system. In *Systems, Process & Control (ICSPC), 2013 IEEE Conference on* (pp. 306-309). IEEE.

Yuksekkaya, B., Kayalar, A.A., Tosun, M.B., Ozcan, M.K. and Alkar, A.Z., 2006. A GSM, internet and speech controlled wireless interactive home automation system. *IEEE Transactions on Consumer Electronics*, *52*(3), pp.837-843.

Zhai, Y. and Cheng, X., 2011, August. Design of smart home remote monitoring system based on embedded system. In *Computing, Control and Industrial Engineering (CCIE), 2011 IEEE 2nd International Conference on* (Vol. 2, pp. 41-44). IEEE.

YOUR KNOWLEDGE HAS VALUE

- We will publish your bachelor's and
  master's thesis, essays and papers

- Your own eBook and book -
  sold worldwide in all relevant shops

- Earn money with each sale

Upload your text at www.GRIN.com
and publish for free